WHAT'S RIGHT ABOUT YOUTH MINISTRY

Six Values Great Youth Ministries Embrace

By Mark Oestreicher
with responses from Kurt Johnston

Reading Schedule:

September 15 – September 22	*Introduction & Chapter 1*
September 23 – September 29	*Chapter 2 & Chapter 3*
September 30 – October 6	*Chapter 4 & Chapter 5*
October 7 – October 13	*Chapter 6 & Chapter 7*
October 14 – October 20	*Chapter 8 & Chapter 9*
October 21 – October 27	Reflect on Homework

WHAT'S RIGHT ABOUT YOUTH MINISTRY
Copyright © 2018 by Mark Oestreicher

Publisher: Mark Oestreicher
Managing Editor: Sarah Hauge
Cover Design: Adam McLane
Layout: Marilee R. Pankratz
Creative Director: Stuart Smalley

All rights reserved. No part of this book may be reproduced in any form by any electronic or mechanical means including photocopying, recording, or information storage and retrieval without permission in writing from the author.

Scripture quotations marked (NIV) are taken from the *Holy Bible*, New International Version®, NIV®. Copyright © 1973, 1978, 1984, 2011 by Biblica, Inc.™ Used by permission of Zondervan. All rights reserved worldwide. www.zondervan.com. The "NIV" and "New International Version" are trademarks registered in the United States Patent and Trademark Office by Biblica, Inc.™

Scripture quotations marked (NLT) are taken from the *Holy Bible*, New Living Translation, copyright © 1996, 2004, 2007, 2013, by Tyndale House Foundation. Used by permission of Tyndale House Publishers, Inc., Carol Stream, Illinois 60188. All rights reserved.

ISBN-13: 978-1-942145-40-0
ISBN-10: 1-942145-40-3

The Youth Cartel, LLC
www.theyouthcartel.com

Email: info@theyouthcartel.com

Born in San Diego
Printed in the U.S.A.

CONTENTS

Introduction: 2005, then 2008, then 2012, then Today	7
PART 1: SO MUCH AWESOME	11
Chapter 1: The Secret Sauce of Great Youth Ministry	13
Chapter 2: Four Points of Light	31
PART 2: SIX VALUES GREAT YOUTH MINISTRIES EMBRACE	45
Chapter 3: The Long View	49
Chapter 4: The Power of Small	57
Chapter 5: The Role of the Holy Spirit	65
Chapter 6: Integration over Isolation	73
Chapter 7: Embracing the Role of Parents	81
Chapter 8: Contextualization	95
PART 3: OKAY, SO...	101
Chapter 9: Intentionality Moderated with Faith and Humility	103
Appendix: A Homework Assignment	112

This book is intended to be an encouragement, and the most deeply encouraging of all our peers is Scott Rubin. Scott, this is for you.

INTRODUCTION: 2005, THEN 2008, THEN 2012, THEN TODAY

Way back in the early aughts (the 2000s, that is), many of us who had already taken several laps around the youth ministry track started getting concerned about many of the models and assumptions we'd practiced for years. As one of many who were actually training other youth workers, I was even growing uncomfortable with some of the things I was saying in seminars I was leading.

Adding greatly to this discomfort was data surfacing in some of the first legit research being conducted on the efficacy of youth ministry and the realities of adolescent faith development. Honestly, the brutal truth I was facing was that *at least some aspects* of what I'd been promoting to other youth workers was purely rooted in my assumptions, and that *at least some of those assumptions* were, in fact, false.

I started spending a good bit of time thinking about this gap. At the time, I was the president of Youth Specialties, and had the annual opportunity to do the closing main session talk at the National Youth Workers Convention. For three years in a row, I developed and delivered what I could only think of as "shots across the bow," attempting to sound the alarm and articulate what was wrong.

In 2005, after the third of those talks, the YS publisher encouraged me to write it up as something of a manifesto of change, which resulted in the publication of *Youth Ministry 3.0: A Manifesto of Where We've Been, Where We Are, and Where We Need to Go*.

Problem was, by the time the book released in 2008, I already disagreed with some of the content I'd written. I felt that I'd done an acceptable job of naming the problem; to this day I stand by the framework suggested in that book, which named the search for belonging as the lens through which today's teenagers view their world and their own development (in other words, "Where I find belonging will tell me who I am"). But I had real issues with the "Where we need to go" part of the book. I, and others, strongly felt that part was coming across as an upper-middle-aged white dude with a programming mindset suggesting potential new options that were merely repackaged versions of the same ol' thing. And it felt that way, probably, because I *was* an upper-middle-aged white dude with a programming mindset suggesting potential new options that were merely repackaged versions of the same ol' thing. Really, I didn't know what was next, but felt pressure to get practical.

About a year and a half later, I lost my job at YS during an ownership transition. And shortly after that, Group Publishing came to me and said, "We want you to write something for us—what do you want to write?" I remember my response word-for-word: "I've been wanting to write *Youth Ministry 3.1: What I Wish I'd Said*." They were stoked, and off we went. In the end, as it was a different publisher, and probably not all that healthy to merely write a reactive book to a book I'd previously published, we decided to reframe that new work into *A Beautiful Mess: What's Right About Youth Ministry*. And that book was released in 2012.

This time around, following the book's publication I wanted to change less, but I still thought I hadn't nailed it—at least not when it came to the book's organization. As I started speaking on the content of that book, what I wanted to say evolved into some content I've since become passionate about. Through seminars and teaching I came to call this content *Six Values Great Youth Ministries Embrace*. And, in a sense, that's what you're now reading.

After a nice five-year run, Group's book went out of print and the rights to the work reverted to me. I still loved this content and thought it was helpful for youth workers, so The Youth Cartel decided to revise and expand that previously published work. I asked my buddy Kurt Johnston—whose pushbacks on the pessimism of *Youth Ministry 3.0* were a major factor in setting the optimistic direction of *A Beautiful Mess*—to write chapter responses, and he graciously agreed.

If the timing of this cycle continues, I should be deeply frustrated with this book in a few more years, and begin thinking then about writing a reaction to it or another revised version.

Marko, May 2018

Part One

SO
MUCH
AWESOME

CHAPTER 1: THE SECRET SAUCE OF GREAT YOUTH MINISTRY

I'm a pot-stirrer.

I have carved out a little niche in the youth ministry world by being a contrarian. I have spoken, written, taught, preached, and conversed until I'm blue in the face about our need for change in youth ministry.

There was a "youth ministry must change or die" vibe to my blog for years. And in the last decade-plus, all kinds of amazing research has come out to support my "windbaggedness."

- Christian Smith's research in the National Study on Youth and Religion created a tipping point into angst for thousands of youth workers; his identification of Moralistic Therapeutic Deism as the primary faith of American teenagers (Christian or not) rocked us. Kenda Dean's brilliant follow-up to this study, *Almost Christian*, framed the bleak issues with a sole focus on Christianity.

- An oft-quoted Southern Baptist survey (among others) showed teenagers leaving the church and their faith at a rate of up to eighty percent (other surveys, by other groups, revealed tempered—but still startling—results).

- Chap Clark told us that teenagers are deeply Hurt, and we all knew—even if we didn't verbalize it—that our rah-rah youth group approaches weren't addressing that pain and isolation.

- The Fuller Youth Institute's *Sticky Faith* research was more upbeat, as it provided proactive steps. But the unspoken implication was clear: What we've been doing does not promote a faith that lasts.

- Even my own book, *Youth Ministry 3.0*, made the case that most of us are framing our youth ministry thinking and approaches around a culturally outdated priority of need for autonomy, when the dominant need of today's teenager is belonging.

As I crisscrossed the country speaking to and with youth workers, and as I interacted with them via phone and email and Facebook and blog comments, I heard a growing sense of depression. My primary work these days is leading a yearlong coaching program for youth workers, and through it I've benefited from a courtside seat to the inner thinking and practices of roughly 450 youth workers' insecurities, questions, and longings. Sure, there are arrogant youth workers who are convinced they're doing well because they "have the numbers to prove it." But the average youth worker these days—at least among those who read youth ministry books and articles and blogs—seems to have a looming sense of malaise: "I still love teenagers and feel called to them, but everything I read tells me I'm failing."

That's a difficult place to minister out of, that feeling of missing the mark.

Despite chipper reminders from optimists like Kurt Johnston (of Saddleback Church), pleading with us that "the youth ministry sky is not falling," there's a black cloud overhead for many youth workers.

This book is not a 180. I'm not going to stop pushing for change. I will continue to rant and write manifestos. I will continue to poke the bear.

But I've also experienced a bit of a perspective shift. During my decade at Youth Specialties, I certainly had contact with a multitude of youth workers. However, I can see in hindsight that my role put me in a bit of a silo (or some other metaphor that would be the ministry organization equivalent of an academic ivory tower). In the past nine years, in my work with The Youth Cartel, I've had so many more long conversations with in-the-trenches youth workers. I'm overstating this, but I feel—in some ways—that I've become reacquainted with real youth pastors.

This move from the executive suite to the street has brought me face-to-face, over and over again, with the daily contrasting realities of pain and hope that real youth workers live with. And I've been reminded of the good stuff. I mean, I never left youth ministry (I've been a volunteer small group leader at my church for twenty years), so I knew the good stuff of living into my calling and having great conversations with teenagers and the joy of doing youth ministry with other servants. But I was a bit too focused on the part of the glass that's empty, the black-cloud stuff.

So, no, this book isn't refuting what I've ranted about before or what I will, surely, say in the future and later want to rant about. Instead, this is my small attempt to describe the goofy, awkward, messy beauty in the full part of the glass (whatever percentage it is).

There's a subtle arrogance (and I've definitely fallen prey to this) in thinking that we've blown it. That might sound strange, because an honest acknowledgement of where we truly have missed the mark requires a massive dose of humility. But often embedded in much of the conversation about how to "fix" youth ministry (I'm calling myself out here) is the unspoken idea that I am capable, and that you are capable, of transforming the lives of teenagers. The thinking is: if teenagers don't embrace a robust faith, and it was because I wasn't doing youth ministry right, then if I change things up, I can cause them to be more Christian.

Along the way, we've often misplaced the gorgeous value of patience.

The mundane way of steadfastness.

The unflashy path of consistency.

We forget what we've taught our teenagers, over and over again: that God often uses the most improbable and unskilled to do his most amazing work.

The Samaritan woman who met Jesus at the well (John 4:4-26) understood almost nothing about who Jesus really was or the living water he offered her. She was a Samaritan (despised by Jews), and a woman in an almost exclusively patriarchal culture. She'd had five husbands and was living with another dude (sin!). But she was the first missionary, proclaiming her story with simple words (John 4:29, NIV): "Come see a man who told me everything I ever did. Could this be the Messiah?"

Before he met Jesus, Matthew, author of the Gospel book, was among the most hated of all people—an evil, swindling tax collector, buddies with the worst of the worst sinners, traitor to his people, instrument of oppression. He became a disciple of Jesus.

Peter, of course, was a hotheaded loose cannon and a nobody. But then Jesus said, "Upon this rock I will build my church" (Matthew 16:18, NLT).

Even minor characters throughout Scripture fit this pattern:

- Simeon, the old dude hanging around the temple, recognized the baby Jesus as the Messiah and had the opportunity to pray over him and bless him (Luke 2:25-35).

- David's Mighty Men, before anyone referred to them that way and before they participated with God in jaw-dropping feats straight out of the best action movies (2 Samuel 23:8-23), were a bunch of losers—distressed and in debt and discontented (1 Samuel 22:1-2).

- The kid with the weird little lunch of loaves and fish got to participate in one of the greatest miracles ever, feeding an entire amphitheater of people (John 6:1-15).

- Even Mary, mother of Jesus, was a teenager with no prominence, no particular standout ministry skills.

We've told these stories to teenagers as examples of how God wants to use even them. So shouldn't it make sense that God wants to use even us? Even you? Even me? And doesn't it follow that God will work through us to draw teenagers to himself, whether we have brilliant youth ministry skills or not, whether we have the right approach or not?

A modern-day story was shared with me recently by a friend of mine, gifted veteran youth pastor Sam Halverson. Sam had a teenage guy in his group (we'll call him Tim) who'd shown no spiritual interest whatsoever and was normally brooding and dark in his outlook. At a particular worship time, the students in Sam's group were given some space to reflect on their spiritual lives. Tim sat by himself and was drawn into a very personal something. Sam couldn't tell what was going on, whether Tim was having a profound spiritual moment, or was angry, or something else. He noticed Tim with his head down; as Sam moved around the room and neared Tim, he could tell Tim was in the midst of something intense. Sam said he had no idea what to do. Should he interrupt what was possibly a personal moment between Tim and God and ask Tim what was going on? Should he lay hands on Tim and pray for him? Should he leave Tim alone?

Sam, feeling helpless and bumbling, lightly touched Tim on the shoulder and quietly said, "I'm here." Tim nodded but said nothing. As he walked away, Sam felt he'd probably blown it and that there was likely something better he should have done (though he had no idea what that better thing would have been).

A week later, Tim's mom called Sam about another issue. At the end of the call, she said, "Oh, and I wanted to tell you thanks for what you did for Tim." Sam was confused. Tim's mom continued. "Tim told me that he was really struggling with whether or not God even exists. In that prayer time, Tim was begging God to reveal himself. He prayed, 'If you're real, God, then do something—right now—to say "I'm here!"' Tim told me that the second he prayed that, you put your hand on his shoulder and said, 'I'm here.'"

The fact is, Sam is a great youth worker. He's smart and relational and creative and caring. But that moment with Tim had nothing to do with Sam's youth ministry skills. Sam felt like he'd blown it! But God was working through Sam and in Tim.

Maybe the glass is more full than we realize. Maybe the sky isn't falling.

THE OPTIMIST'S PUSHBACK

All of this perspective reorienting has me asking a few hard questions (questions I can hardly believe I'm asking, because they're so imbued with optimism, even if it doesn't look that way):

- What if all our tweaking and trying to fix the broken

system is actually creating a problem bigger than the one we're trying to solve?

- What if our pushing and tweaking are merely masking our lack of dependence on God, or our own Messiah complexes?

- What damage will be done if we spend the next twenty years in youth ministry replacing one methodology with another methodology?

- What if we're asking the wrong questions?

- What if this whole youth ministry thing is simpler than we make it out to be?

WHAT'S THE POINT OF YOUTH MINISTRY?

A youth ministry friend of mine recently asked me a version of this question, but he phrased it this way: "What's the single objective of youth ministry?" Questions like that scare me, because as soon as I offer a response, I think of another possible answer.

I like complexity and abhor easy-answer theology. Identifying a "single objective" of anything is tough, because we always have multiple objectives—always, whether we want to or not. I'd be so much more comfortable with a list of objectives than singling one out.

But…
On this question, I'd like to play ball. And I'm gonna use

one word to answer it: Christlikeness. That's our singular objective. If I were to put it into a sentence, it would be something like: "The single objective of youth ministry is to walk with teenagers on their journey toward Christlikeness."

Of course, there are a ton of secondary objectives implied in my sentence (as is—did I already write this?—always the case). For instance, we can't merely say, "The objective is discipleship" without addressing what we mean by "discipleship."

My role as a youth worker is to honestly live my own journey toward Christlikeness with and in front of the teenagers in my midst. I can't change teenagers—that's the Holy Spirit's job. I'm not directly in the transformation business; **I'm in the transformation-hosting business**. Hosting is a metaphor that brings up sub-metaphors like steward ("How do I steward the time I have with teenagers in a way that best exposes them to the transforming work of the Holy Spirit?"), curator ("How can I highlight and bring attention to the good stuff God is already doing in the world and in the lives of teenagers?"), and evangelist.

Wait—did I just write evangelist?

Yup—but I don't mean it in the way you might think. I mean it in the same way that Apple might have an evangelist on staff (an iPad evangelist's job is to share the good news about iPads). My role as a youth worker is to be the evangelist for teenagers in my church. I am the lead banner-waver for teenagers in my congregation (or one of the banner-wavers, since I'm on a team), reminding people in the congregation of their responsibility to collectively engage with the teenagers in their midst.

IS YOUTH MINISTRY BIBLICAL?

There's been a small-but-loud rash of pushback on youth ministry in recent years, suggesting that it's unbiblical. In many ways, it's rooted in an understanding of a Bible passage.

The Shema is Israel's most important Scripture. God-fearing Jews, to this day, pray the Shema first thing when they wake up and last thing before they go to sleep.

> *"Hear, O Israel: The Lord our God, the Lord is one. Love the Lord your God with all your heart and with all your soul and with all your strength."* (Deuteronomy 6:4-5, NIV)

Christian theologian and author Scot McKnight has proposed we embrace the same practice, adding a line from Jesus, "Love your neighbor as yourself," and calling it *The Jesus Creed*.

But the next two verses in Deuteronomy contain the bits being used as an argument against youth ministry:

> *"These commandments that I give you today are to be on your hearts. Impress them on your children. Talk about them when you sit at home and when you walk along the road, when you lie down and when you get up."* (Deuteronomy 6:6-7, NIV)

Actually, Deuteronomy 6 refers to parents and their children a few times. This is one of the primary places in Scripture that we see the responsibility of parents clearly laid out in terms of the spiritual formation of their kids. It's a good, biblically sound argument.

But this movement goes way beyond passionately calling parents to step up in terms of leading their children and teenagers spiritually. The movement suggests that youth ministry is unbiblical because it isn't mandated in the Bible. At a recent event on these issues, a youth ministry friend of mine shared the stage with a guy whose official title was "Youth Ministry Abolitionist." Wow.

Let's list a few things that are common in our churches today that aren't listed in the Bible:

- Baptismal pools and fonts
- Church buildings
- Hired clergy
- Church budgets
- Church buses and vans
- Sound systems
- Children's ministry
- Men's ministry
- Women's ministry
- Senior adult ministry

That list could easily be ten or a hundred times as long, right? And those aren't bad things. They are contextual approaches to doing church (which, for the record, is not quite the same as being the church).

In one sense, of course, there's no directive about youth ministry in the Bible. Adolescence, while always existing (contrary to popular myth—see Crystal Kirgiss's excellent and fun book *In Search of Adolescence: A New Look at an Old Idea*) in both developmental and culture ways, has taken on unique shaping realities with the rise of modern youth culture. So adolescence was much less of a cultural issue when the Bible was written. And yet, we can still see plenty of examples in Scripture of other adults (not the parent of the child or young person) playing a significant role in the faith development of a "youth." For example: Samuel and Eli (1 Samuel 3). But looking for a biblical directive is somewhat beside the point.

The church is called (see: the New Testament!) to share the gospel and grow disciples, to be the presence of Christ on earth. In a world where youth culture exists, this simply must include adults who are cross-cultural missionaries, willing to embody the gospel into that cultural context. If we're not willing to do this, we're not being the church.

Hear me: this does not mean that I think we should consistently remove teenagers from their parents and wall them up in isolated spaces with only their peers (and a few crazy adults willing to get pizza stains on their shirts and dodge dodgeballs). But it doesn't have to be an either/or situation.

We can *both* be engaged in ministry to and with teenagers *and* support parents in their role of spiritually leading their children.

All of this assumes we're interacting with parents who give

a rip, of course. There's plenty of important youth ministry to be done with teenagers whose parents are completely disengaged. I know I'm preaching to the choir here. Not too many Youth Ministry Abolitionists will be reading this book.

I was going to move on now, but I feel compelled to write a bit more from my personal experience.

First, I wouldn't be where I am without the loving input of youth workers in my own life. My parents are amazing. They're godly people, loving parents, and were very engaged in my life. We spent lots of time together, and they actively modeled their faith in front of me on a daily basis. No, they weren't perfect, but they were everything we would hope teenagers would have, and more.

And yet I needed, and my parents were glad for, other adults speaking into my life.

Fast-forward. I am a parent of two young adults. Riley is currently 24, and just graduated from college as I write. Max is 20 and in the midst of college years. I love my kids, and they're a very high priority in my life. We love being together, and we hang out all the time. I regularly speak into their lives, draw boundaries, encourage competencies, talk about faith stuff, and do multiple other things we all hope teenagers would get from their parents. I'm far from perfect. But I was humbled and encouraged when my church's youth pastor told me I'm a great dad (and even more so when my own kids tell me that).

Would my two children, when teenagers, have been okay if my church's youth ministry didn't exist? Maybe. But time and time and time again, I have been thankful for both paid and volunteer youth workers who loved Riley and Max, spoke truth to them, provided a safe place for them to be honest about questions and screw-ups, and encouraged them toward Jesus. I could not be more thankful for the youth workers from my church and their role in my kids' lives.

Yes, more than a youth worker, I am a parent who is thankful for youth ministry. I'm fairly certain your church is full of parents like me.

THE THREE COMPONENTS OF GREAT YOUTH MINISTRY

Have you ever said something, off the cuff, then realized that there was more truth to it than you even intended? That happened to me a few years back.

I was in Orlando, speaking at the e625 convention (an international convention for Spanish-speaking youth workers). I love these events. After attending many of them in Argentina and Guatemala, I hadn't been to one in a couple of years, and I'd missed it. The energy is higher than at the youth worker conventions you may have attended. The attendees are noticeably un-jaded. They are genuinely eager. And that's infectious.

I was teaching a two-and-a-half-hour *super curso* on my book *Youth Ministry 3.0*, of course with a translator. I'd barreled through the cultural creation of modern youth culture, the extension of adolescence (both the beginning and the end points), the three tasks of adolescence, and the shifting prioritization of those tasks. The standing-room-only group in the room was totally engaged and asked fantastic questions. Their body language was all "I'm in." So, I should have closed it out with a handful of suggestions and packed it up.

But with about fifteen minutes to go, I had a sense. Call it the Holy Spirit, call it reading something subtle in the responses, or call it—more likely—just stepping outside of myself for a moment and noticing how passionately I was speaking (hyping?) this stuff that was, to one extent or another, merely my opinion and conjecture. I had this sense that I was burdening my Latin American youth-working friends with a bunch of technology that they didn't need. (I'm using technology in the broadest sense here, meaning the systems and methodologies and scaffolding we construct and perpetuate.)

I stopped. I said:

Let me be clear about the three things that are necessary for great youth ministry:

1. *You like teenagers.*

2. *You are a growing follower of Jesus.*

3. *You are willing to live honestly in the presence of those teenagers you like.*

After I said it, I thought to myself, "That was actually true!" It had a sense of surprise to it.

Do we need more theological reflection in youth ministry?

Yup.

Do we need to rethink our assumptions and practices? Sure.

Do we need to study the changing face of the teenage experience and adjust accordingly? Yes.

Do we need a revolution in youth ministry? I still think so.

But what we don't need is to replace one technology ("programs are the answer!") with another technology ("post-programming is the answer!").

What we need—and this is why I've always felt that some of the best youth ministry happens in small churches with zero technology—are:

- Adults who like teenagers.

- Adults who are actively growing in their own faith.

- Adults who will live authentically in relationship with those teenagers they like.

I can hardly believe I'm writing this, but there really is a magic formula—a math equation—for great youth ministry:

*A grace-filled caring adult who's willing
to be present with teenagers*

\+

A small-ish group of teenagers

\+

The power of the Holy Spirit and presence of Jesus

=

Fantastic youth ministry!

I'm going to keep harping and ranting and instigating. But I can't get caught in the trappings of a "new way" of doing youth ministry, and I hope you don't wander down into that dead end either.

KURT'S RESPONSE

Over the course of our long friendship, Marko has described me in all sorts of ways. He's called me Pollyannaish, overly optimistic (a kinder way of saying I'm Pollyannaish), pragmatic, and practical, and said I'm a guy who has never seen a half-empty cup of water. He once asserted that I'm such a fierce utilitarian, I don't see the need for anything that can't be easily implemented in a ministry setting. In this chapter, he reached into his bag of Kurt descriptors and pulled out a new one: chipper. To all of these charges I plead a hearty, "Guilty as charged!" (except being a Pollyanna...that one's just plain mean). I think our differences are what have made our relationship a great example of iron sharpening iron—we see things differently, we lead differently, and we do ministry differently. Marko does things in a thinking sort of way; almost nothing he does is void of good thinking. I sometimes remember to think as I do things. Ain't nobody got time for too much thinking. There's ministry to get done!

So, as I write these little responses at the end of each chapter, I hope you will sense my deep love and respect for my friend. I'll give some hearty 'Amens' and I'll push back and offer other perspectives, and I'll do all of it hoping this book helps you think about and do the amazing work of youth ministry in such a way that your efforts make a dent for God's kingdom and his glory.

What do I like about this first chapter? Umm…all of it! But I'm especially glad to see one of youth ministry's deepest thinkers willing to cut to the chase and simplify things out of the gate. I couldn't agree more with his mathematical equation (the youth ministry I lead uses a similar one in our training materials) because it's important to have a simple, solid foundation of youth ministry upon which to build.

There are lots of ways to approach youth ministry; please don't let the so-called experts speak more authoritatively into your ministry than they deserve. You know your students, you know your community dynamics, you know your church's theology and values (please tell me you know your church's theology and values!). So take everything you learn in workshops, listen to in podcasts, and read in books like this with a grain of salt.

But Marko's mathematical equation for youth ministry? You can take that to the bank.

CHAPTER 2: FOUR POINTS OF LIGHT

The earliest youth workers in modern youth culture (post-World War II) were zealous relationship-jockeys. The church—for the most part—had its head in the sand when it came to this new thing of youth culture, quickly chalking it up as an evil passing fad. But the missional impulse of early youth workers wouldn't let them settle for that kind of dismissal. With a strong sense of calling, a glorious sense of clueless adventure, and a helpful little rebellious streak (hmm, sound anything like youth workers today?), these beta testers forged their own way, often without the support of the church (and often, to be honest, in the face of resistance from the church).

Their primary *means* of doing youth ministry? Building relationships with real teenagers in the real world of teenagers. And that meant cross-cultural movement.

Andy Root, in his scary-true book, *Revisiting Relational Youth Ministry*, points out that many of us have been using relationship building as a manipulative tool to coerce teenagers into our desired outcomes. I must, with significant discomfort, admit that this practice has been way too present in my own youth ministry journey.

But let's assume there have always been scores of youth workers who aren't manipulative results-junkies like I have been (at times). One thing I've seen quite clearly over these past several years of super-heightened communication with hundreds of youth workers is this: most youth workers (counter-intuitively, this applies particularly to those who haven't done the reading and attended all the training events) operate from a beautiful place of pure relational ministry. That's a strong statement, one that might invite some frowns from my cronies in the world of youth ministry thinkers.

I have argued and screeched about the need to return to the relational impulses of our youth ministry forefathers and foremothers. But I think I had it wrong (at least partly). Where I was right is that most of the youth ministry machine (training, resources, ideas, experts) has—for a few decades—focused more on programs and models. For them (for us), we do need a return to non-manipulated relationships as the central impulse and practice of youth ministry.

But most youth workers never left that assumption or practice!

Every week, it seems, I meet in-the-trenches youth workers—underpaid servants whose names you've never heard, and volunteers who don't know who I am—who do this because they genuinely like teenagers. They're not particularly savvy. They often possess an overreliance on pragmatism ("I've just gotta make it through this week's youth group"). But they are, in a word, pure. They have skirted the missteps of the youth ministry glitterati for the past few decades because they either don't know the experts exist, they don't have time to listen to the experts, or they simply don't care (and I mean that as a compliment).

Maybe you, like me, are one of the *minority* who got caught up in all the distractions: big events, attendance-boosting elixirs, the awesomest Spotify playlist ever, super-slick images on your worship screens, or the relentless temptresses, "what's new" and "what's next."

And if so, maybe you, like me, need a multiyear course of detoxification and deprogramming.

But what if you're reading that and thinking, "Huh?" Well then, good for you. Return to your previously scheduled program of spending time with teenagers, being present with them in the midst of their joys, fears, and questions, and introducing Jesus into the mix. That's what you've been doing, and it's what you should continue doing.

Here's some quick-and-dirty anecdotal observational analysis. Not long ago, I spoke at four weekend youth retreats over a six-week stretch. At the first three, I had a blast, connecting with teenagers during my times of speaking and while walking around. I saw youth workers of every stripe sitting with students in the main session and during meals, walking around with them, laughing, praying—being in relationship. But at the fourth event, things were different.

Things were going OK according to the program, and I hadn't had any overt resistance to the message I'd been asked to bring. But I could sense—even from the stage, in the midst of speaking—a standoffishness, a resistance, a disconnectedness. And I noticed: none of the hundred adults who are there were actually hanging out with the teenagers. During the main sessions, the teenagers were seated in rows and the adults were hanging out (often talking) at round tables in the back of the room, behind the soundboard. A similar pattern was seen during the meals.

I'm sure I'm exaggerating a bit, and that there were some wonderful youth workers at that event who give and give themselves to teenagers. But during my final morning talk, I specifically looked and could not find one single adult seated among the teenagers. This is the glass half empty.

But the glass half full is that on three out of four retreats, amazing relational stuff was happening all over the place! Sometimes I miss the good stuff happening all over the place in youth ministry because of the places of struggle.

Really, there is so much positive movement in the world of youth ministry these days. I'd like to point out just four of these positive-movement realities.

LONGEVITY: AN UPSIDE OF THE INDUSTRY OF YOUTH MINISTRY

Before you become totally convinced that I'm biting the hand that feeds me, or naively denying my own culpability in the development and propagation of the approaches perpetuated by "the industry of youth ministry," let me call out a wonderful, glass-half-full trend.

Professional youth ministry, for years, was merely seen as a stepping stone to the ministry big-show (senior or associate pastor roles). Youth pastors were, in essence, pastoral interns, putting in time and cutting their teeth. And while the conventional wisdom that the average tenure of a paid youth worker was a year and a half may have been nothing more than an urban myth, anyone who's been around the block a few times in youth ministry has seen the damage caused by a revolving door of youth workers at a particular church.

And that, thankfully, *has changed* (mostly, I must add, as a positive result of the professionalization of youth ministry). With organizations like Youth Specialties and Orange (and many others) saying, "Youth ministry can be a lifelong calling," youth workers around the nation are staying put.

A veteran youth worker used to be anyone who'd stayed in the game for five or more years. Seven years was impressive. But today, it's not uncommon in the least for me to meet youth workers who've been at it for fifteen or twenty years. I'm still impressed when I meet thirty-year or forty-year vets (mostly because they had to choose to stay in youth ministry back when it was still viewed by most as a rite of passage to other roles). The lengthening of the average youth ministry stay is a massive win—for churches, for teenagers, for parents, and for the kingdom of God.

Case in point: in one of my coaching cohorts right now, five of the ten participants have more than fifteen years of experience each. That percentage was unheard of a decade ago.

Honestly, not all that much can be accomplished in the first couple of years at a church. The really good stuff usually doesn't happen until year three. And I simply get all bubbly inside when I talk to youth workers who tell me, "Yeah, I've been at the same church for twelve years." *Those* people, they get to live the good life. They have volunteer teams of former students, even teenagers whose parents had the same youth worker. They are less impacted by criticism (and usually receive less of it), aren't usually in a battle over under-communicated expectations, and are often icons of steadfastness in their churches.

I find such great and life-giving encouragement in this trend toward longevity. And while I occasionally hear horror stories of veteran youth workers being pushed out of their churches because the church thought "someone younger was needed," the general directional movement is good. It's cause for celebration. Let's raise a half-full glass of whatever toasting liquid you prefer both to youth workers who stay put and to those rookies who have a vision for longevity.

E'RYONE'S GOT A VOICE: RESOURCING EACH OTHER GOES VIRAL

For decades, roughly two organizations had a monopoly on youth ministry training and resourcing (of course, this was in addition to various denominational efforts). I worked for one of those organizations. And I'm not saying those organizations were bad, or did a bad job of training and resourcing youth workers. It's just that the pipeline of thinking (resulting in training and resources) was very, very narrow. That can lead to sameness.

Today, big youth ministry serving organizations are struggling to find their footing. Tectonic plates have shifted. Organizations sold and merged and rebirthed. Honestly, the big dogs aren't such big dogs anymore.

Of course, this crazy little thing called the Internet happened. Thanks to that new reality (and, I'm sure, a host of other factors), culture moved from monolithic to tribal. And even in our little youth ministry pond, in-the-trenches youth workers started to find a platform to share their knowledge, opinions, and ideas. Youth workers started resourcing each other.

Some of these "little guys" were entrepreneurial and didn't long for a position at one of the legacy organizations. Instead, they started their own thing. And today, I'm constantly hearing about or discovering a new small business or ministry eager to serve youth workers.

This, my friends, is a great thing. It might be a challenge at times to find exactly what you need, but there sure are a lot more options out there!

Even the organization I'm a part of (The Youth Cartel, which published this book) is a tiny, scrappy effort with no office and a sense of pride about how small and powerless we are.

Not that irregularly, a younger youth worker will ask me some form of the question, "How do I get where you are?" Well, the answer to that question a dozen years ago would have been a difficult pill to swallow: luck and God's providence. But today, the answer is "Just start doing what you want to do; put it out there, and see if God is in it!"

THOUGHTFULNESS AND THEOLOGICAL REFLECTION

There's been a cliché stereotype of youth workers floating around, especially in evangelical churches: the immature but energetic party planner. Those exact words might not always be used, but the image of a ringmaster (at best) or Peter Pan (at worst) would quickly resonate if you mentioned it to the average churchgoer.

At least, that would have been true fifteen years ago.

And, as much as I hate to admit it, the cliché was not completely unwarranted. But there's been a shift, a really significant one. It might not be completely obvious to everyone in every church, but the shift has traction.

My sense is that youth workers, on average, tend to be pragmatic. The senior pastor might have time and inclination for extended periods of closed-door study and reflection, but youth workers leaned toward action. This is likely due to a combination of factors:

- The expectations of churches
- The personalities of most youth workers
- The examples we've observed of the youth workers before us

But maybe the biggest reason for this historic leaning toward pragmatism and action lies in our collective perception about what great youth ministry entails. I mean, if *the ultimate game* is the goal (I'm using a little hyperbole here, but not much), deep thinking isn't all that needed. If the job is mostly about organizing transportation and having Cokes with teenagers, theological reflection seems pretty low on the list of priorities.

But there's been a significant shift in this arena, and it's awesome.

Youth workers—thousands of them—are starting to look beyond game books and topical curriculums. Youth workers are thinking deeply, asking difficult questions, wrestling with complexities, and engaging in theological reflection. Holy cow.

A few anecdotal examples:

- When I was choosing a college, in 1952 (no, I'm kidding; it was 1981), I knew I was headed into youth ministry. But I couldn't find a single college with a youth ministry major. Sure, many had a course or two, but I couldn't find an official major (maybe one existed, but I didn't find it). Today, there are more than a hundred colleges and universities in North America alone with majors or minors in youth ministry.

- And that youth ministry higher education I just referred to is going through a major transition. Those majors and minors at Christian colleges and universities were often, in their early days, focused on a combination of basic skills and social science. But many programs are shifting their focus to understanding spiritual formation.

- Getting a teaching job at one of these colleges or

universities used to only require a master's degree and some number of years of experience. But today, it would be very difficult to become a youth ministry professor without a doctorate (meaning, there are scores of qualified candidates with a PhD or a DMin).

- The Association of Youth Ministry Educators (AYME) and the International Association for the Study of Youth Ministry (IASYM) are flourishing independent academic bodies supporting the advancement of deep thought and research in youth ministry. Both organizations support academic journals—the *Journal of Youth Ministry*, and the *Journal of Youth and Theology*— each of which have peer-reviewed articles.

- Youth Specialties/Zondervan, Baker Books, IVP, and other publishers have chosen to publish deep and thoughtful youth ministry books (some of them full-on academic) over the last fifteen years.

- Major youth ministry training events like the National Youth Workers Convention added theological topics to their seminars and panel discussions. The presenters are actual theologians, the topics are as meaty as meaty can get, and the response from attendees is strong.

- The Princeton Forum on Youth Ministry is an annual event with topics that have a theological depth completely unheard of twenty years ago.

- Real, credible research in youth ministry is being conducted in quantities never seen before.

- Blogging and podcasting have provided a platform for robust thinkers in youth ministry—often people without publishing and speaking bullet points on their résumés—to wrestle publicly with deeper issues.

I could list another dozen examples, easily, but you get the idea. There's been an unmistakable shift toward thoughtfulness and theological reflection in our field. That's a very, very good thing.

EXPLOSION OF YOUTH MINISTRY GLOBALLY

Amazing, innovative youth ministry is now flourishing on every continent. Certainly youth workers in the States weren't the only ones doing youth ministry in previous decades. But the development over the last decade of indigenous models and training and resource organizations around the world gives me great hope that the global church is maturing in its efforts with teenagers.

An example: fifteen years ago, there was next to nothing available in terms of training, resources, or encouragement for Latin American youth workers. Today, the organization e625 publishes dozens of books each year, holds an international convention, and holds national events in more than a dozen countries, in addition to having grass-roots teams in twenty countries. As I write this paragraph, I'm in Ecuador, having just spoken at two national events here in the last couple days, one in Guayaquil, and one in Quito.

Organizations like Youth Hope provide training to youth leaders in the developing world, taking care to not force

American assumptions and models on different cultures, but helping leaders develop culturally responsive ministry approaches to reach the teenagers in their own countries.

The youth ministry world is truly becoming a global family of people who share the same calling.

KURT'S RESPONSE

First, I think Andrew Root and Marko are being a little tough on our collective historical reasoning for relational ministry. To say that it was "a manipulative tool to coerce teenagers into our desired outcomes" makes me really, really uncomfortable. I can't bring myself to assign generations' worth of youth workers such motive. Having said that, of course we have an ulterior motive for hanging out with teenagers! A thirty-five-year-old spending time with teenagers with zero ulterior motive is creepy and concerning (although, their ulterior motive can be creepy and concerning, too, I suppose…). So, if spending time with teenagers with the "desired outcome" of them ultimately coming to faith in Jesus Christ is wrong—I don't wanna be right. Okay, I got that off my chest.

Second, as an optimist, it's hard for me to see the downside to some situations. But since my overly chipper, Pollyannaish friend is pointing out four points of light, I'd like to offer a word of warning for each.

Longevity: An Upside of the Industry of Youth Ministry

I couldn't agree more with Marko on this amazing trend, which I hope isn't merely a trend, but a long-lasting norm. But there is a downside to the professionalism of youth ministry and the long-term youth careers it has fostered: comfort. The fear I have for all of my career-minded youth ministry friends is the very same fear I have for myself and have forced myself to check on a regular basis: that comfort would creep in, that I would become soft, that I would lose my edge, that I would get in a rut...even if it's a pretty good rut. The fact that our generation of youth workers may not be forced to explore a "real ministry role" at some point might cause us to settle in and assume youth ministry is all God has planned for us. While I certainly hope more and more folks feel called to long-term youth ministry, I hope we remain open to his nudge to other areas, too.

E'ryone's Got a Voice: Resourcing Each Other Goes Viral

True! But when everybody's an expert, nobody is. As an entrepreneurial-minded person, I see this new explosion as exciting and wonderful, with almost unlimited possibilities for anybody to share insights, input, encouragement, and resources with the rest of the youth worker world. We no longer have to spend a thousand dollars traveling to a three-day conference to learn from others and sharpen our saws. But, just because somebody has a voice doesn't mean you need to listen to what that person says, nor does it mean that person's insights are as valid as somebody else's. These days almost everybody has something to say and thinks he or she is the person to say it. When people ask me if the timing is right for them to write their first book, or try to speak at a training event, my input is always the same: Do you have something to say? Are you the person to say it?

Thoughtfulness and Theological Reflection

The only downside to this is the tendency for some folks to overthink it. As you become more thoughtful and theological in your approach to youth ministry, never forget the simplicity and power of Marko's little mathematical equation.

Explosion of Youth Ministry Globally
No downside to this!

Part Two

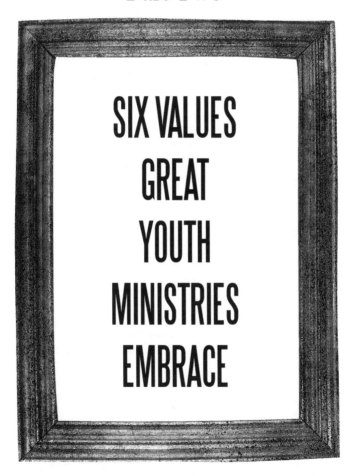

SIX VALUES GREAT YOUTH MINISTRIES EMBRACE

When I wrote an earlier version of this book (published in 2012 as *A Beautiful Mess: What's Right About Youth Ministry*), I pointed out a very short list of bright spots on the horizon. Like flower buds pushing up through the dirt in the spring, they were emerging trends, potential reasons for hope.

In the years since then, I've taught on these ideas, refined them, added to them, and seen them move from being emerging bright spots to values that great ministries embrace. In fact, the subtitle of this book is based on this section, as I've seen that great youth ministries in every corner of the country (and many other parts of the world) are embracing these values.

I'd even go so far as to write that when I see thriving youth ministries these days, they are always intentionally or unintentionally working to embody most of these values.

So what do I mean when I use the word *value*?

Here's how we teach it in our Youth Ministry Coaching Program:

Mission ("Why do we exist?")
↓
Values ("What are we called to embody in this season?")
↓
Strategy ("How will we embody the values?")
↓
Goals ("What action steps and measurements do we need to know if we're embodying the values?")

In other words: why we exist (leads to) what we're passionate about (leads to) how we'll embody this (leads to) how we'll know if we're succeeding.

I've become confidently convinced that ministry growth (in whatever way you define that) comes from identifying those values that are more aspirational ("We want to value these, but if we're honest, we don't yet"), and coming up with intentional strategy for leaning into them.

Values are the key to a vibrant youth ministry (well, Jesus is the key, but you know what I mean). In fact, I'd suggest that discerning values and coming up with strategy for embodying them is one of the most important functions of leadership in any context, with leading a youth ministry being no exception.

So while I spend a good amount of my time helping youth workers understand a process of collaboratively discerning their own ministry values, I'm going to spend the following six chapters unpacking values I see being embraced by vibrant ministries all over the globe. They're not in any particular order, and are often quite different from each other. But here's what I'd like you to do as you read:

1. Prayerfully consider which of these six values your ministry is already embracing. Might as well give yourself a little pat on the back where you can!

2. Then, I'd love to have you prayerfully consider which *one or two* of these six would make the biggest difference in the health and vibrancy of your ministry, were you to come up with strategy and goals for moving them from aspirations to realities.

CHAPTER 3: THE LONG VIEW

The humble youth worker knows and lives a ministry approach that actively practices faith in God to transform lives, knowing we are powerless to change hearts.

More than twenty years ago, a job change at my church was leaving me less connected to teenagers. The new role had some awesome challenges and opportunities for growth, but I knew I'd be running on fumes quickly if I lost all interaction with the people God called me to. So for fairly selfish reasons, I identified three incoming seventh grade guys in my junior high ministry and asked them if we could hang out. Specifically, I asked them if they'd be willing to do something of a devotional on their own, three days a week, then meet together on Sunday night at Taco Bell to talk about it. None of them were extroverts or already stepping into leadership. But I could tell they were intelligent and thoughtful (for seventh grade guys!).

Thankfully, all three said yes, and we met together weekly for the next two years. We quickly developed safety and a value of honesty with each other. We talked about the Bible, theology, doubts, being a seventh-grade dude, living for Jesus, and a hundred other topics. I think back on this little group as one of my many fond memories over my thirty years in middle school ministry. Just as those guys finished junior high, I moved to San Diego and fairly quickly lost touch with them (this was long before Facebook!).

And I would like to think that these three guys got just about the very best of what a church could hope to offer junior high guys—our focused and intentional discipleship and mentoring, in addition to all the other awesome aspects of our church's flourishing junior high ministry.

One of those three guys was Michael. Let me tell you a little of his story, most of which I didn't know about until many years later.

Just as his freshman year of high school was beginning, Michael had a traumatic head injury from a skateboard accident and was incapacitated for three months. There should have been immediate support and relational contact from that church's high school ministry, which had multiple paid staff and a solid system of small groups. But somehow, Michael fell through the cracks. And other than a Get Well card, Michael felt somewhat abandoned by his church.

After his doctor cleared him to resume normal life, Michael returned to church on a Sunday morning. He entered the high school ministry room, feeling somewhat anxious, and confused by the lack of contact he'd received over the past few months. He told me (years later) that while a couple people said hi, not one person asked him where he'd been or how he was, or expressed that they'd missed him. A switch flipped, and Michael suddenly, in that space (remember: he was a fourteen-year-old ninth-grader at the time), concluded that he didn't belong, that church was a joke, and that all Christians were hypocrites. And he never came back. That ten minutes in the back of the high school ministry room was Michael's only interaction with that ministry.

Super intelligent but bored with school, Michael dropped out after his sophomore year and got his G.E.D. His dad co-signed on a loan and Michael opened a skateboard shop, which failed. At eighteen, Michael moved to Las Vegas and settled into a fairly self-destructive lifestyle (involving everything you'd likely imagine). For a number of years he sort of drifted through life. He said he never really dropped his belief in God, but he was very angry at the church and had concluded God was, at best, distant and impersonal.

After a dozen years, Michael decided to get himself together. He dropped many of his destructive habits, and got a job at an accounting firm. Being as bright as he was, he succeeded and received multiple promotions. At twenty-seven and a half years old, Michael examined his life and thought, "I've really got a great life. Good job, nice car, a great condo, a pretty girlfriend." But he sensed that there was one glaring unresolved area—this nagging question of whether his fourteen-year-old self had been right about the church. He was pretty sure he'd concluded correctly, but felt a need to re-address the whole issue in order to put it to rest for good.

Michael decided to attend church one more time. He chose

a church in a way that many of us would not like to think would work: he saw a billboard.

By this time, Michael had tattoos up and down his arms. He purposely wore a sleeveless shirt that morning, as an intentional dare to whoever would look at him funny or say something negative about his ink. He parked in the farthest corner of the large church's parking lot, hoping and expecting to have a negative interaction (even a judgmental look) with someone prior to reaching the church, so he could turn around and go home.

But the first person he encountered smiled and said, "Great tats, man. Who does your work?"

That was it. Michael was back.

Here's what I find stunning about this story. The actions that caused Michael to leave, and the action that opened the door to his return, were so very, very minor. They weren't about structures or methodologies or programming or curriculum or buildings or youth rooms. They were both—negative and positive—about expressing (or not expressing) a sentiment: "You belong, and we want you here."

Amazing. Seems life a puff of air—something so featherweight. But in negative and, thankfully, redemptive ways, these seemingly minor expressions shaped Michael's story more than anything else over the last two decades.

My family was in Las Vegas on vacation a year and a half later, and Michael reached out on Facebook, asking if we could have coffee. That's where he told me this whole story.

By this point, Michael was a high school ministry small group leader at that church, and very committed to his faith.

As he was telling me this story, I was distracted. I had long told other junior high youth workers: "Junior high ministry doesn't have good feedback loops. You can't judge your success by how teens look when they're in your ministry. You have to judge your success by how they look when they graduate from high school." (Or, I sometimes said "when they're twenty-one.")

If I'd measured our success with Michael when he was eighteen, he would have been a check mark in the failure column. At twenty-one: still a failure check. Twenty-four? Fail. Twenty-seven? Fail, still. It wasn't until he was twenty-seven and a half that Michael reconnected with God and the church. As he was telling me his story, I very briefly thought to myself, "I have to change that point in my training to "we have to measure our success by how they look when they're twenty-seven and a half." Then I quickly realized that was stupid. I was using an entirely misguided and wrongheaded set of assumptions.

Michael is a reminder to me of the importance of The Long View.

God drew Michael back, not me or his new church. But the Sunday evenings I spent with Michael (and Ben and Garrett) at Taco Bell, sharing our lives and talking about the Bible, remain a critical part of his story.

The truth is that God was pursuing Michael *long before* he entered our junior high ministry and my two years with him.

God continued to pursue Michael through his thirteen years of wandering. And God will continue to pursue Michael for the rest of his life. As much as we might try to control the beliefs and behaviors of teenagers, we're powerless to transform lives. That's God's role, not ours. Of course, I don't desire that any post-youth grouper walk away. But their stories and their journeys are not mine to control. All I can do is be faithful in the here and now while trusting God for each teenager's future.

The Long View leans into humility, trust, and hope.

> *And this hope will not lead to disappointment. For we know how dearly God loves us, because he has given us the Holy Spirit to fill our hearts with his love.*
> (Romans 5:5, NLT)

KURT'S RESPONSE

I'm a fan of Jesus' parables, even though they can oftentimes be tricky to interpret (side note: If we get to have a Q&A with Jesus someday, my first question will be, Why were you so clear in your teaching sometimes, and so stinking confusing other times?). One of my very favorites is the parable of the sower who threw seed on four types of soil, found in Matthew chapter 13. If you do the math, Jesus seems to be indicating that only about twenty-five percent of the "soil" is good soil, ready to receive and grow the seed. If you translate this parable into your youth ministry setting, suddenly things become a whole lot less frustrating. Every teenager who walks through your church doors is in a different place spiritually; the soil isn't all the same.

I don't think our job is to try to figure out which teenager is "good soil" and which isn't. Our job is to sow, sow, sow, and sow! God's job is to work on the soil.

So, what does this have to do with having a long view? Everything! Focusing too much on immediate, measurable results is a dangerous game, and one that is almost impossible to win. The world is full of Michaels, young men and women who attended amazing junior high ministries before wandering for a while. My hunch is that Marko could tell dozens of such stories. So could I. You probably have a few of your own. When Michael wandered away from the church and his faith, it would have been very easy to put the youth group's ministry to him in the "loss" column. After all, if they had done a better job of walking alongside him during his injury and recovery he certainly wouldn't have wandered, right? Who knows! We can't predict the decisions our students will make and the paths they will choose to walk, and evaluating our effectiveness by their decisions is a recipe for an early exit from ministry.

The world is full of Michaels, many of whom are still wandering. But their story isn't over; hard soil can become fertile. Just ask Michael.

CHAPTER 4: THE POWER OF SMALL

Since small churches often don't have the resources to develop impressive programs fueled by amazing technology, they are often forced to "settle" for the core of what really works in youth ministry: a caring, Jesus-following adult engaging a small group of teenagers.

I grew up in a big church, with a big youth ministry. The smallest church I worked in had about 700 in Sunday attendance, and the other churches I worked in ranged from 2,500 to 8,000. Much of this was because I was passionate about junior high ministry, and only larger churches tend to have the budget for a specialist in that area.

But I think I subconsciously developed a line of thinking that big churches were better than small churches—particularly when it came to youth ministry. I couldn't conceive how a small church, without "adequate resources" and paid staff, could really deliver when it came to the complexities of programming a great youth ministry.

What an idiot, right?

I remember, not that long ago, feeling a bit disoriented when hearing Mark Yaconelli (a brilliant youth worker and author of many books, including *Contemplative Youth Ministry*) tell me about his own experience of youth ministry. While Mark's dad, Mike Yaconelli, was one of the godfathers of modern youth ministry and the co-founder of Youth Specialties, Mark grew up in a tiny church of thirty people. Mark said, "We didn't have a youth ministry. My experience of youth ministry was Stu, the guy who genuinely and authentically asked me how I was, every week."

I was confronted with my lousy thinking on this several years ago when I spoke at two youth events on subsequent weekends. The first event was a statewide denominational event in Arkansas. It was a good event, and I don't remember having anything other than positive impressions while I was there. I do remember (though this might have been in hindsight) that there seemed to be a high percentage of good looking, extroverted, and popular kids—certainly all those involved up front fit that description.

The next weekend I was speaking at a very similar, though somewhat smaller, event for a few districts (smaller sections of a state) of the same denomination, but in a part of Virginia marked by smaller cities and towns. I was standing on the side of the main session during the worship time, prior to my first talk, looking at the faces of the teenagers as part of my spiritual preparation for the work I was about to do. And I noticed a few things in very rapid succession:

1. "Wow, there are a lot of misfits here. I see a bunch of handicapped kids. I see overweight kids, and teens with bad acne, and students whose haircuts simply hint that they don't have a lot of social options."
2. "All of these misfits are completely engaged in worship. They are unashamed and not hiding."
3. "This is beautiful."

These misfits had clearly been told, "You belong, you matter, we want you here."

I instantly choked up and started to fight back unwanted tears. And then I was introduced to speak. I made my way to the stage and struggled, as I was still in the midst of fighting back tears. And I couldn't exactly say, "Sorry, it's just that you guys are such losers, and it's so beautiful!"

I pulled myself together and made it through that first talk, then spent the next day or two trying to figure out what was going on. I asked the organizers all sorts of questions (that were, I'm sure, mildly off-putting). Eventually, talking with the event's registrar, I noticed something unique. This event was primarily populated by small youth groups, five to ten teenagers per group. There was one *slightly* larger group (something like twenty), but most were little groups.

All weekend I heard youth workers say things like, "We don't really have a good youth ministry. It's just me and Luanne over there, and we have dinner with the teenagers on Sunday night and talk about Jesus." Or, "We don't even have a youth ministry. This event *is* our youth ministry, and the three kids we brought are just a part of our church, normally."

I'm not suggesting that big churches have bad youth ministry and small churches automatically have great youth ministries. But I am suggesting that the pathway to great youth ministry is *shorter* in small churches.

What I've noticed is that some of the best youth ministry takes place in small churches. Of course, that statement requires us to unpack what I mean by "best." Certainly, when looking at churches without all the bells and whistles, many youth workers (particularly those who have access to the bells and whistles) would assume that nothing good can come out of Nazareth ('cause it's small and backwater). "Sure, they're trying, but there's no way they can pull off the creativity, complexity, and competence we embody." (Some big church is going to pick up those three "C" words as its tagline, just watch.)

Here's my observational insight: small churches are often blessed into wonderful youth ministry by their very lack of resources. In fact, I'm becoming more and more convinced that one of the worst things that can happen to a youth ministry is for it to become well resourced. If small churches had resources, they might have gone down the same paths of distraction and bluster that have plagued so many of us.

There's been amazing research about adolescent faith development in the past fifteen years. Two of the most important studies (from my perspective) were the National Study on Youth & Religion (headed by Christian Smith, and reported in many books, including Kenda Dean's maybe-the-most-important-youth-ministry-book-ever, *Almost Christian*), and the Sticky Faith research out of Fuller Youth Institute. At the risk of significantly oversimplifying the findings of these studies, here are three absolutely critical conclusions:

- Parents make a bigger difference than we youth workers do, by far (more on that later)
- Teenagers need to be part of the congregation, not isolated (more on that later also)
- Teenagers need to verbalize their faith much more than they need to be told what to believe

What size church tends to naturally live into these statements? Not all small churches live into these truths well, but they occur more naturally in smaller churches, *because of* their lack of resources.

Resources (budget, space, staff) aren't evil. In fact, they can be pretty darn helpful. But I see that over and over again, resources can become a seduction, tempting us to trust them for transformation and results.

If you're in a smaller church (let's say 300 people or less), thank God for your lack of resources. Thank God that you may not have had your hand forced to pursue fantasticality. Count it a blessing that your only option may have been to "compromise" on what you could do and "settle for" spending time with teenagers without impressing them.

If you're in a midsized or larger church, watch out for those resources; they bite. Watch out for how they seduce you and threaten to control you. Pay attention to your level of excitement over budget approvals (this could be your "canary in a coal mine," warning you that it's time to redirect your energies). If you're in a midsized or larger church, you have to be that much more intentional about embracing a value of small, making it the core DNA of your youth ministry approach. Remember, there's a mathematic equation for great youth ministry that we looked at earlier:

> A grace-filled caring adult who's willing
> to be present to teenagers
> +
> A small-ish group of teenagers
> +
> The power of the Holy Spirit and presence of Jesus
> =
> Fantastic youth ministry!

KURT'S RESPONSE

My senior Pastor, Rick Warren, is fond of saying, "The only people who like big churches are pastors," and I often wonder if the same is true with youth groups. Food for thought, for sure.

Hidden in the middle of this chapter is one of the more profound youth ministry observations I've encountered. "I'm not suggesting that big churches have bad youth ministry and small churches automatically have great youth ministries. But I am suggesting that the pathway to great youth ministry is shorter in small churches."

I have to admit that as a big church youth ministry guy, I've always assumed the cards were stacked in our favor; what could be wrong with having an abundance of just about everything that makes youth ministries tick? Volunteers? We have extras. Budget? Ours is larger than that of most churches. Parent involvement? We have to turn them away. Meeting space? Yep, with room to spare (apologies to all of you who constantly fight with the senior adult quilting ministry for a room). But guess what we don't have? We don't have a short path to the stuff that really matters! In fact, it's because of all our resources and options that we constantly feel the need to remind ourselves of what really matters. We have to work incredibly hard to make sure our youth ministry is allowing students to experience the stuff that so naturally happens in smaller settings.

If you happen to lead a larger youth group, don't apologize for it and don't buy into the false narrative that big means shallow, that "attractional ministry" was the Devil's idea (hopefully, I'll find someplace in a future chapter reply to climb onto my "attractional vs. missional" soapbox). But if your youth group is only big, and isn't intentionally marked by some of the qualities and characteristics that make smaller youth groups so powerful, you are missing the whole point. A large youth group that isn't also small in the ways that count really isn't a youth ministry at all.

> *Try to follow the guide but still listen for the Holy Spirit.*

CHAPTER 5: THE ROLE OF THE HOLY SPIRIT

Great youth ministries are more responsive than proactive, more about discernment than planning, all with a keen ear to the unique guidance of the Holy Spirit.

One shift that, perhaps, gives me more gut-level hope than any other is the awakening I'm seeing in youth workers across the country to the Holy Spirit.

I've had a bit of an awakening to the Holy Spirit myself in the last couple of years. As soon as most people read that sentence, though, they will assume I mean that I've awoken to signs and wonders stuff. That's not what I mean. (Everything on the table: I'm in the middle. I'm not a cessationist, but I've not had much personal experience with or desire for signs and wonders experiences.) The awakening to the Holy Spirit that I've experienced has played out on two levels: in my own life and faith practice, and in my thinking about youth ministry and church leadership.

My last year at Youth Specialties, back in 2009, was marked by the pressure I felt to perform for our corporate parents. It was particularly soul-deadening for me. By the time I got laid off, I was close to burnout—both professionally and spiritually. But in the two or three months that followed, I experienced a gorgeous reawakening of my soul. I felt God's presence for the first time in a long time. My prayer life rekindled, and I started to hear God speaking, nudging, consoling.

I knew this was the Holy Spirit, who had never left, of course. Instead, my spiritual eyes were merely opening to the Spirit's presence.

This ramped up when I launched the Youth Ministry Coaching Program. When my cohorts were in times of personal sharing, I started sensing the Holy Spirit giving me insight that was beyond me, and I even started receiving what could only be called words of truth to be offered to others. I entered into the exercise of this with open hands— not grasping it or claiming it or being arrogantly confident about whatever I might think I should say. But I was amazed, over and over again (as I have continued to be over the past eight years), that what I was hearing—from the Holy Spirit—was usually accurate. One of the most powerful of these experiences was a time when I had a strong sense that another person in the sharing circle had a word from God for the person talking. I had no idea what was going to be said, but sure enough, when I called that out, the words spoken had a profoundly holy and truthy beauty to them, and we all knew we were on holy ground.

This awareness of the Holy Spirit has changed both my

regular, everyday experience of God as well as my youth ministry practice. When I'm leading my middle school guys small group, for example, I'm trying to choose (and it is a choice, by the way) to simultaneously listen to my guys and to the Holy Spirit. One of the surprise benefits to me, in a youth ministry setting, is that I feel unburdened and free. That's because I'm not carrying the absurd responsibility of being smart or insightful enough to know what to say.

This personal awakening and shift in my practice has also shaped my thinking about youth ministry and church leadership. If you ever hear me talk about *Youth Ministry 3.0* stuff these days, I hope you hear the difference from what I wrote about in that book. When I wrote that book, more than ten years ago now, I was not operating with this mindset or experience, and most of my suggestions in it only tip a hat to the role of the Holy Spirit. But these days, I'm convinced that great youth workers (and great church leaders) need to recover the art of collaborative discernment.

Great youth ministry takes all different forms because it has to be contextual. But the path to a wonderfully contextualized youth ministry is not merely an effort of assessment and study. In fact, it is first and foremost an exercise in listening (and I believe that listening needs to be practiced in community, which is why I am passionate about collaborative discernment).

Yes, we need to do assessments and learn about the community in which we do ministry. Yes, we need to read and study and observe. But more important than all of that is the intentional act of gathering a small group of spiritually-minded people to actively listen to the Holy Spirit. Ask,

"What teenagers have you placed in our midst?" (No, just observing them is not enough.) Listen. Ask, "What teenagers are you calling us to in our community?" Listen. Ask, "What would be a culturally and contextually appropriate approach to reaching those teenagers?" Listen.

Bottom line No. 1: without a sense of the Holy Spirit's role in your life, you will always be limited in your own spiritual growth and practice and, therefore, in your youth ministry efforts. Bottom line No. 2: A youth ministry that's not informed by active and intentional listening to the Holy Spirit will miss out on who and what God is calling it to be.

> Here's a strong statement: *Your best youth ministry will never come from excellent brainstorming; your best youth ministry will always be the result of stepping into God's dreams for your ministry.*

Look, I'm not against proactivity or planning. That would just be stupid, or lazy. But I know this:

My worst weeks with my junior high guys small group are the weeks when I'm not prepared. Having no plan and passing it off as allowing the Spirit to lead you is like sitting in a parked car expecting the steering wheel to take you somewhere. Or trying to steer a boat when the engine is turned off. I sense the Spirit's leading much more—particularly in the midst of youth ministry practice—when I'm moving.

My second-worst weeks with my junior high guys small group are the weeks when I have a plan, but am inflexible. I push through with my agenda, not listening to the prompts from God that would lead me to be responsive to what my guys really need in the moment.

My best weeks with my junior high guys small group—and this is *always* true—are the weeks when I'm prepared, but flexible. I have a plan, but I'm intentionally listening and watching for a nudge from the Holy Spirit. In fact, this is really the spiritual art of youth ministry: learning how to tell when that kid's comment or question is the Spirit saying "Go there!" and when it's just that guy being a distraction, or experiencing indigestion from his latest burrito.

Honestly, there's a lot I don't understand about the Holy Spirit. But I know these three statements to be absolutely true:

- God has dreams for your youth ministry (and for every teenager)
- The Holy Spirit is actively at work
- We're invited to join in

Other than charismatics and Pentecostals, most of the American church has ignored the third person of the Trinity for decades—but that's changing. We need more of this, because we need more of the Holy Spirit. We need to embrace humility, prioritizing spiritual responsiveness over brilliant planning.

KURT'S RESPONSE

The Holy Spirit has always confused me. I think it's because I'm drawn to simplicity and easily tangible ideas and practices. I've been called lots of things in my life, but nuanced and mysterious are two words nobody would use to describe me. Yet those are the two words I'd most often use to describe the Holy Spirit. This is certainly part of what often makes me uncomfortable when the topic comes up. Another likely factor is that I grew up in an overly Pentecostal church where the Holy Spirit seemed to only be interested in making people speak in a strange language, knocking folks off their feet or causing them to perform in numerous other strange ways when summoned. These days I serve on staff at a Southern Baptist church, where there's no threat of a Holy Spirit sighting!

Given my history, you can imagine my hesitancy recently when I was invited to speak at a large gathering of junior highers on the topic of, you guessed it, the role of the Holy Spirit in the life of Christians. How would I teach an arena full of seventh and eighth graders about something I can't quite reconcile myself?

Then I saw it. I'd seen it a thousand times before, but had never paid attention. Maybe the Holy Spirit isn't as mysterious and nuanced as I've always believed. Perhaps the role of the Holy Spirit in our lives is tangible, even simple.

In John chapter 14, Jesus describes the soon-to-arrive Holy Spirit in simple language: as an advocate and a helper. That description jumped off the page as I read it, and suddenly my task of helping explain the mysteries of the Holy Spirit to a bunch of junior highers became far less mysterious. There's a lot I can't explain about it all; I still carry some baggage from the ways the Holy Spirit has been misrepresented in my past. But I'm done running and I'm done pretending I can experience all of God while simultaneously ignoring one third of the Trinity.

The Holy Spirit as my advocate, as your advocate, as the advocate of the kids in our ministries? Seems simple enough.

The Holy Spirit as my helper, as your helper, as the helper of the kids in our ministries?

There may be no more tangible role for God to play.

CHAPTER 6: INTEGRATION OVER ISOLATION

We'll see long-term faith more often when we work to decrease the constant ghettoization of teenagers and help them find meaningful belonging in the life of the church.

Somewhere along the superhighway of youth ministry professionalization, many of us bought into the idea that it's in the best interest of teenagers, in terms of spiritual development, to separate them from the rest of the congregation. In many ways we were just mirroring our culture, which has progressively moved toward almost complete isolation of teenagers from the world of adults over the last fifty years.

Many of the problems I'm addressing in this book are connected. Here's a short list of interconnected factors that are all both chickens and eggs:

- The isolation of teenagers

- The increasing infantilization of teenagers (treating them as if they are children)
- New brain research showing that teenagers' decision-making brain parts are underdeveloped being interpreted as a disability rather than a divinely-intended opportunity
- The swing to helicopter parenting
- The loss of public spaces where teenagers are allowed to hang out together
- The lack of jobs for teenagers that involve interaction with adults in the world of adults

All of these factors are working together to negatively impact teenagers in myriad ways.

And then there's this little bit of cynical observation: isolating teenagers in our churches *feels like* a win/win/win:

- It feels like a win for the teenagers themselves, who would seemingly (so we think, at least) prefer to hang out in a homogeneous grouping than get stuck with a bunch of old farts.
- It feels like a win for professional youth workers, because it justifies the existence of our jobs, making us more and more indispensable.
- It feels like a win for many of our congregations who *really do* want teenagers to grow in faith and have a good experience of church, but would rather not have to interact with them. It's easier to show our support by financing a professional and an isolated youth group than by actually being involved with teenagers.

Teenagers today live almost their entire day-to-day in an isolated bubble with only their peers. They spend a big chunk of their time in school, where the only adults (however pure and noble teachers' motives may be) are those who are paid to be with them, in the world of teenagers. In off-school hours, they're hanging out with peers (IRL or online), playing sports (with peers), or working at a starter job where they are likely supervised by a twenty-something in extended adolescence.

The phenomenon of extended adolescence is directly tied to this isolation. In our culture, teenagers no longer have an opportunity to spend time with adults in the world of adults. As a result, they never have a chance to be an "apprentice adult." Compare this to 100 years ago (not that I'm interested in idealizing that era or returning to it!), when older teenagers and young adults spent the majority of their time living and working alongside adults, learning by observation and "trying on" what it means to be an adult. On-ramps to adulthood have been almost completely shut down, and young adults are left to their own difficult explorations about how to take responsibility for their own lives.

Sadly, we've done the same thing in the church. In our march to perfect the youth group, we've often isolated teenagers from adults in the church, or any opportunity to engage and be engaged by the church at large. No wonder teenagers have no idea how to make the transition from youth group to the larger church when they graduate!

Again, Christian Smith's research, and Kenda Dean's application of that research for the Christian church (in the book *Almost Christian*), helps reveal the problems of this approach. Sensing a meaningful connection and belonging to the larger church body (and not just the youth group) is one of the few prime indicators of a church engagement that outlasts adolescence.

But there's movement. I meet youth workers every week who are wrestling with this problem. It's not an easy one, particularly in a church where there's a long-established tradition of isolating the teenagers. People don't tend to like change.

Youth workers across the country are experimenting with breaking down this isolation. Youth workers and churches are taking baby steps in the right direction.

One of the many practical examples of some early awakening to this challenge is the trend by many churches to shift toward intergenerational mission trips (as opposed to youth-only mission trips).

And while I'm not suggesting you do this, as I don't know your context, I've seen quite a few churches making the bold move to discontinue high school Sunday morning programming (Sunday school), because they realize teenagers no longer attend two hours, and they'd rather have the high schoolers actively participate in the main church service. (By the way, this is best accomplished with a concurrent effort to *involve* teenagers in the church service.)

To be extra clear: I hope it's obvious that I'm not lobbying for the discontinuation of age-specific youth ministry in churches (go back and read that bit about whether or not youth ministry is biblical, in the first chapter, if you're not clear on this). Teenagers still need safe places to be their authentic selves in relationship with peers who are wrestling with the same issues. But age-segregated youth ministry and integration don't have either/or approaches. It *should be* a both/and commitment, with a priority on finding ways to move toward integration. The best youth ministries, those that are really thriving (and by that I mean creating disciples who continue in faith beyond their years in youth group), are finding creative ways to embrace integration.

(Final note: the best book on this is Sam Halverson's book, published by The Youth Cartel, called *One Body: Integrating Teenagers Into the Life of the Church*.)

KURT'S RESPONSE

One thing is obvious: my church loves teenagers. They even built a twenty-million dollar building on the farthest corner of the property, 300 yards away from where the adults congregate, as a symbol of their affection! When the new youth center was unveiled, momentum, budget, and attendance all increased at a shocking rate. Youth ministry at Saddleback Church had never been better.

And then I read the research Kara Powell and the Fuller Youth Institute revealed in their book, *Sticky Faith*, and my world was rocked. Among a host of other findings, their research identified intergenerational relationships as a primary contributor to a teenager's journey with Jesus. While these relationships don't have to happen within the church, the church is a natural environment for such relationships to occur...if we let them. And for the most part, we weren't. Don't get me wrong, we weren't philosophically opposed to the adults of our congregation rubbing shoulders with teenagers, but outside of the obvious roles they could play in our youth ministry we weren't doing anything proactive and intentional to allow the paths of the older and next generations to cross. Something had to change.

I dubbed my plan "Project Mix." It consisted of three key strategies:

1. **Cancel youth gatherings one weekend per month (in our setting, our youth group church service occurs simultaneous to the adult service), and allow (force) teenagers to attend the adult service.** And so, Worship Together Weekends (catchy name, I know) were born—and they went over like a lead balloon. "Why in the world would we let a massive youth center sit empty twenty-five percent of the time?" "Why in the world would teenagers want to attend church with the adults?" "Why in the world would Pastor Rick want a bunch of rowdy students invading his sanctuary on a monthly basis?" The fact that it was my wife asking these questions didn't boost my confidence. But I was convinced that our teenagers needed to know, and be known by, the adults of our church and this seemed like a good place to start. We are several years into the Worship Together Weekends journey, and we are still trying to get it right. Being intentional in designing a church service with adults and teenagers in mind is tough. But it's worth the effort…I think, anyway.

2. **Look at the various activities we do in isolation, and see if we can do them with the adults instead.** We used to do a student version of our church membership class, so we shut that down and started encouraging teenagers to attend membership class with the adults. We had a variety of community service events we were participating in as a youth ministry one weekend, and the adults would do the exact same event the next weekend—so we combined efforts. We looked for ways to encourage adult small groups to adopt student small groups and include them in their activities

once in a while. We've had some successes and lots of failures in this arena, but where it has worked, it has worked well.

3. **Find as many student-friendly ministries as possible.** For years, the only areas our students served in were kids ministry or our own youth group. As part of "Project Mix," I talked to dozens of ministries within our church to determine if they were open to allowing teenagers to join their teams, and the result was overwhelmingly positive. We now have teenagers on our adult audio team, playing with the adult worship bands, greeting first-time guests, and so much more.

We still have a long way to go to make "Project Mix" the success I dream it can be. But we are taking baby steps, we are eating the elephant one bite at a time, and we are crawling before we run (and a whole bunch of other analogies!).

CHAPTER 7: EMBRACING THE ROLE OF PARENTS

Great youth ministries are passionate about helping parents—the key influence on teenage faith—succeed in their God-given roles.

Some years ago, Mark DeVries published a book called *Family-Based Youth Ministry*. Whether Mark intended it to or not, his book—even the presence of the book, and the title alone—opened a crack in the pervasive thinking that we can effectively minister to teenagers while ignoring their parents.

Mark's book wasn't the only force promoting this idea. Many others were spreading the same message. Christian Smith's research (mentioned at the beginning of this book) conclusively proved what was logical but largely ignored: parents are the single biggest influence on teenagers' faith. Smith went so far as to say (I'm paraphrasing), "If you want to see what a teenager's faith will look like in adulthood, look at his or her parents' faith."

81

Across the board in youth ministry—across denominations and geographies—youth workers are now taking seriously the call to engage with parents as a critical aspect of youth ministry. Seeing youth workers understand family systems and at least attempt to encourage parents in their significant role has become more normative than exceptional.

If we're being honest, there's an embedded tension in this truth for most youth workers. Most of us didn't get into youth ministry because we were passionate about coming alongside parents. Most of us don't wake up each day thinking, "How can I hang out with parents of teenagers today? Because that will give me life!" Nope: we got into youth ministry because we dig teenagers. And in light of the never-ending list of relationships that need attention on the radar of most youth workers, spending time with parents means *not* spending time doing other things, like hanging out with teens.

But to be true to our calling, we've simply got to do this. And when we do, we often see fruit.

FIVE TRUTHS ABOUT PARENTS OF TEENAGERS

How about I offer you five insights—five truths—about parents? I'm not suggesting I've got every aspect of parent ministry nailed. But I do have three things going for me:

1. I've been involved in the practice of youth ministry for a very, very long time. Heck, I've been in youth ministry longer than some parents of teens have even been alive!

2. I've watched thousands of youth workers succeed and fail with parents.
3. I've been a parent of two teenagers, who are—as of this writing—twenty and twenty-four years old. I was not the youth pastor at my church during my own kids' teenage years (though I was a volunteer in the junior high ministry), so I got to view youth ministry from the perspective of a parent.

Parents are not the enemy. This one should be obvious. There was a time in youth ministry when it wasn't as obvious, and youth workers regularly spoke about parents as if they were the enemy. But those days are (mostly) behind us. Since most (certainly not all) youth workers have not actually been parents of teenagers themselves, there's a natural gap between our experience and that of parents. And it's very natural to assume that we know better; after all, we're experts on adolescence. And we regularly see parents (or hear about parents) "misbehaving" or parenting poorly.

While most of us don't overtly believe that parents are the enemy, our programming, communication, and attitudes often reveal that we hold a deep skepticism about parents' motives and behaviors. When we give space to that skepticism, parents *feel* it, even if only on a subconscious level.

Instead, we must choose to adopt a hopeful perspective toward parents, and a come-alongside set of practices.

Ignoring parents diminishes impact. Man, I learned this one the hard way. More than once, I chose to deal with difficult parents by ignoring them. This almost always made things worse in the long run. And it never once actually improved the situation.

But this truth is about more than handling conflict. The unavoidable truth is that if we don't take parent ministry seriously, we are falling down on our calling, and we're being unfaithful.

Most parents are afraid. Parenting teenagers is *incredibly difficult.* There are constant unknowns and potential pitfalls. There are myriad spoken and unspoken messages and expectations about "how I'm supposed to do this." And many of those messages and expectations just don't feel right, even though they're culturally pervasive.

As a result, I've found that almost all parents are parenting from a place of fear—at least some of the time. The only parents who *aren't* occasionally or regularly parenting from a place of fear are:

- Those who are overly confident (arrogant) and wrongly convinced they've got it all figured out.
- Those who truly don't care, and are disengaged from the lives of their teenagers because their focuses are wholly elsewhere.

Parents of teens regularly wonder if they're "doing it wrong" or screwing up. They fear that they'll be exposed as the clueless parent they often feel like. They fear that their kid will make a massive bad choice that will impact the kid's life, or the family's life, forever. They fear that they're going to mess up their kids, sending them to a lifetime of therapy. They fear that they're doing things that will result in their kids hating them.

Most parents won't admit to you that they're afraid. Most aren't even fully aware of it, as they haven't been honest with themselves about this reality. So their fear sometimes shows up in what we might consider "bad behavior": unfair expectations of you, overly restrictive or overly permissive rules, or even accusations (or questions that feel like accusations).

If you can adopt a curious perspective (really, curiosity is the secret sauce of great parent ministry), situations that might otherwise lead to conflict or tension will be defused. Accusations or tense questions become less personal, less about you, and you're able to function from a place of love and empathy.

Parents often assume an unchanging youth culture. This shows up in two primary ways. First, parents tend to look back on their own experience of being a teenager with either utopian or dystopian lenses. If utopian, they remember their teenage years as the best years of their life (forgetting the hard stuff), and they project that as an expectation onto their teen. They might see their fifteen-year-old emotionally struggling and say something like, "Why are you always moping around? Don't know you that these are the best years of your life!?" (And the kid is thinking, "But my life sucks! If this is as good as it gets, I'm in trouble!") If dystopian, they remember the pain of their teenage years and expect that things will be somewhat identical for their own child.

The other way this truth plays out is that it's fairly normal for parents to assume that the experience of being a teenager in our current context is basically the same as the experience of being a teenager back in the '70s or '80s (or whenever they were teenagers). They realize that social media has brought some changes, but don't think it's much more than that. This is an area where, even if you're a young youth worker without kids, you can help parents. You can help them grow in understanding about the realities of being a teenager today, and how things have changed.

Most parents want help. You might be skeptical about that statement. And I understand why, because it's rare that a parent will reach out and overtly ask for help from you. That's because they've got all that fear! And to verbalize their need for help can subconsciously feel like another indication that *I don't know what I'm doing, and everyone can see that.*

But my experience is that most parents truly do want help—they just don't know how to ask for it. So the responsibility is on us to provide help in a way that doesn't shame them, doesn't *expose* them, and is accessible to them.

FOUR PRACTICES OF GREAT PARENT MINISTRY

I believe there are four practices—you might even consider them "four commitments"—that every youth worker should be living into when it comes to parents of teenagers. When I write *every* youth worker, I mean it: young and not-yet-a-parent all the way through to seasoned and experienced at parenting; volunteer youth workers all the way through to full-time paid youth workers.

I'm a volunteer youth worker with about three hours per week to give to the youth ministry at my church. Most of that time gets taken up with leading my junior high guys small group. So I have very little time left for all the other aspects of youth ministry I'm trying to live into, including parent ministry. But I'm still committed to these four practices. My activity level on these will look very different from a full-time youth worker's, of course, but the commitment to the practices should be the same.

Listen. You may have heard the saying, "Showing up is eighty percent of life" (attributed to Woody Allen). In a similar way, I'd suggest that fifty percent of parent ministry is listening.

When we think about ministry to parents of teenagers, our minds quickly go to programs and initiatives for training and resourcing. We'll get to those, but they're not the lion's share of great parent ministry. The biggest piece of the pie is listening.

Of course, a couple pages back I told you that most parents are afraid. This means that it's more common than not for parents to be unsure of your willingness to listen unless you do two things:

- Communicate over and over and over again that you're available to listen and want to listen
- Focus on the task at hand and give your undivided attention any time a parent takes you up on this offer

Communicate. This one might surprise you, as I'm talking about the effective and regular and clear communication of information about your youth ministry that parents need in order to parent well. Yup, this is partnering well with parents, and it's the next thirty percent of the parent ministry pie (notice: we're at eighty percent of the pie already, and we haven't even gotten to training programs).

A true story: my two kids went to a wonderful and weird little private school (part of the Waldorf school movement). I live in San Diego, but my wife and I grew up in Detroit, and all our extended family are still there. So every Christmas, my family flies to Detroit for the holidays. I use frequent flier miles to book these flights, and since those seats are in high demand over the holidays, I have to book the flights in about July.

When my kids were attending this private school, I'd look at the school calendar online every summer to see if they had posted the fall calendar, including the exact dates of the Christmas break. Every year, the information was not there. Every year, I'd email the school administrator, hoping to catch him in the office over the summer break. Every year, this would be the email exchange:

Me: *Hoping I catch you! I need the dates for Christmas break, and I'm not finding them on the website.*

Him, about a week later: *Oh, sorry about that. We have the calendar finished, but I hadn't posted it yet. Here are the dates.*

Me: *You might remember that I need this information every summer, and it would be great if you could post the dates earlier next year.*

Him: *Sorry, yes, I remember that you asked that. I'll make sure to post them earlier next year.*

We had this exact same exchange every single year for *fourteen years in a row*. I'm not kidding. I don't know if he was a good school administrator or not, but he unintentionally alienated me, caused me to not trust him, and made my job as a dad more difficult. I found myself happy when he resigned.

I wrote this earlier, but parenting teenagers is freaking hard! And the last thing we need is incomplete or inaccurate information. Getting your schedule planned long in advance, getting dates and prices communicated (multiple times)—these are key aspects of parent ministry. When you say you'll be home from the retreat at 3 p.m. on Sunday and you run into a major traffic jam that's going to cause you to be an hour late, you better have a way of getting the word out to parents, or you're choosing to actively alienate them. Great communication builds trust; lousy or late communication destroys it.

Equip. Here's the part you expected—but note that it's only fifteen percent of the parent ministry pie. This aspect of parent ministry can include everything from a parent training event to a resource library to a support/prayer group to a regular email with insights and links (for lots of great ideas, check out Danny Kwon's excellent book, *The Youth Worker's Field Guide to Parents*).

Parents are busy and stressed out in our culture. So the days of offering something that all parents will participate in or use are mostly past us in most contexts. The key is to offer options that will help the parents in your context. Often, this means offering multiple options, allowing parents to opt in to what they have time for and interest in.

As a volunteer with very little time to give to parent ministry, I'm still committed to this practice. My church offers other options (like an annual Parent Summit training day). But since I'm already committed to the previous practice (*communicating*), and send out an email to the parents of the guys in my small group about every six to eight weeks, I always include a little *equipping* in the copy. I'll write a paragraph about middle school development, or share a bit about how junior high guys form friendships, or suggest a book, or share a couple links to online articles I think they might find helpful.

Ask parents what they would find helpful. Experiment. Don't freak out when only twenty percent of your parents attend something you offer (be happy for those twenty percent!). Refine and revise and try additional ideas.

Invite involvement. When I was a parent of teenagers, one thing my church provided that really helped me be a better dad was the opportunity to be involved in ministry to teenagers. Not every parent in your church has the time or gift mix to be involved as a small group leader or camp counselor or food provider. But some do, and offering this option to them is a beautiful aspect of parent ministry (even though it's only the final five percent of the parent ministry pie).

Don't buy into the lie that only young adults should be involved as youth ministry leaders. Having a mix of people, young and middle-aged and old, is always better.

We haven't got this parent ministry thing all figured out yet—far from it. There is still more experimentation, trial and error, and urgency needed. But the movement is undeniable, and that's a very hopeful sign. Vibrant youth ministries are taking this charge seriously.

KURT'S RESPONSE

In my estimation, the most significant development in youth ministry over the past decade or so has been our attitude concerning parents. I think the stages of progression have looked like this:

- Parents are necessary entities to be tolerated.
- Parents are folks we should partner with (meaning, we'll use them when we need to).
- We shouldn't be 50/50 partners; parents are the primary stakeholders in the lives of their children and we should look for ways to support them.
- In addition to the above point, parents are another congregation to whom we can minister. Ministering to mom and dad is perhaps the very best way to minister to a teenager.

I couldn't agree more with what Marko has already written in this chapter, but as a parent of two adult children myself, and as someone who has also been in youth ministry for a long time, I do have a few thoughts I'd like to add. So here, in no particular order, are a few random thoughts and reminders about parents.

- **Today's parents expect individual attention.** I don't wanna pick on my good friend, but Marko's expectation that the school principal change his method of communication solely to accommodate one family's needs is an expectation that wouldn't have always existed. Today, parents expect the rules to be tweaked, the boundaries to be pushed, and the norms to be de-normalized to accommodate their (and their child's) preferences. As a youth pastor, you will live in the tension of navigating when you can, and when you can't (or shouldn't, or simply don't want to), accommodate such requests.

- **Be a bridge-builder, not a wedge-creator.** Each year before our small group season launches, we host a fairly intense day of training for all of our leaders. In this meeting we go through a litany of tips, tricks, guidelines, and best practices. As you can imagine, and have probably experienced yourself, there's no shortage of material to cover when preparing the people who are hoping to invest in the lives of a few teenagers. Buried in all the "stuff" is a little reminder: Never put a wedge between a parent and his or her child. The quickest way to lose parents' trust is by giving them the sense that you don't have their backs–that you are accidently, or even worse, purposefully, undermining their important role. It happens all the time. A junior higher mentions they aren't allowed to date until they are sixteen, and the well-intentioned eighteen-year-old leader rolls his eyes at the audacity of such a lame rule. A high schooler shares that her parents are going to make her pay fifty percent of her car insurance and her small group leader volunteers to talk them out of it. The list could go on and on. Most of the time, our offenses are fairly innocent, and even well-intentioned, but they only serve to hinder our ministry and partnership with mom and dad.

- **The right parents can make the very best leaders.** I'm often asked If I think parents should be allowed to be leaders within the youth ministry, and my answer is always an enthusiastic "Heck yes!" Obviously, some parameters are needed, and there are lots of reasons to turn a parent down, but the right parents can be some of your very, very best leaders. Here are three benefits to parents being leaders in your youth group (there are probably twenty, but I'll limit myself):

1. They are in the trenches like nobody else. Even though they may often feel like less-than-stellar parents themselves, the reality is they are living in the adolescent world 24/7 and bring a ton of fresh insight into your ministry.
2. They have influence with the rest of the church. You are a paid spokesperson for your ministry—and parent volunteers are satisfied customers! Your ministry needs advocates and cheerleaders who have relationships and influence among the rest of your congregation.
3. They have stuff you need. Okay, this one is a little selfish, but the reality is that most parents have a whole bunch of things they can loan your youth group, and are way more likely to do so if they are involved in the ministry. Need to rent a van? Why not ask a parent if you can borrow theirs? Need some tools to work on your stage? Why not ask a dad if he has a few he can loan you? While you're at it, go ahead and ask that same dad if you can borrow his hands.

CHAPTER 8: CONTEXTUALIZATION

In an age of splintered youth culture, great youth ministries have discerned an approach to ministry that is wonderfully unique to their context.

Let me start with this axiom-like observation: everywhere I go in the world, the best youth ministries are always weird. They have a high degree of self-awareness about their uniquenesses, and they celebrate them.

In the modern age, replicating the success of others (whether a burger chain, a software company, or a church) was more than just the norm; it was viewed as the key to improvement and excellence. Sameness, not uniqueness, was the preferential value.

But sameness has shown itself to be both boring and inauthentic, particularly as our culture has swung toward tribalism. Youth culture splintered into thousands of cultures more than a decade ago, and broader culture has followed that lead.

Churches and youth ministries have, for a few decades, looked to examples of whatever ministry they deemed successful and tried to copy as many details as possible. There may have been some logic to this twenty years ago, but it just doesn't fly anymore. And, really, it seems to downgrade vision to "we want to be like that other youth ministry."

The good news: youth ministry copycatting is on the decline, and thriving youth ministries are flying their freak flag! Here are a handful of beautiful truths, pregnant with potential for your youth ministry:

- Your church is unique, even from other churches in your denomination and other churches down the road.

- Your teenagers, while sharing similarities with other teenagers in other churches, are unique. The specific makeup of youth cultures found in your group is unique.

- Your geographical community is unique. Your community has unique values, and your church likely embraces them to some extent, or reacts against them to some extent.

- You, my youth worker friend, are unique in your gifting, experiences, story, passions, and calling. The same is true of the others on your youth ministry team, which means that the vibe and values of your team are one-of-a-kind.

I'm happy that I hear more and more youth workers thinking about contextualization. Youth ministries are starting to ask,

"Given who we are, what we're passionate about, where we are, and the uniquenesses of our context, who is God calling us to be? And how can we develop a youth ministry that embodies that unique calling and is responsive to that unique context?"

You may have used the following line of thinking with your teenagers at some point: God isn't asking you to be *Billy Graham*, or *Moses*, or *Mother Teresa*, or *Chris Tomlin*; God is calling you to be the you he made you to be.

The exact same language of challenge can be used for your youth ministry: God isn't calling you to be just like the youth ministry from that other church, even if that youth ministry is fantastic; God is calling your youth ministry to discern and embody the unique contextualized expression of youth ministry he has dreamed up for you.

Let me help you get started. Wrestle with the following prompts (pro tip: it would be awesome to host a dialogue about these prompts with people from your team, over a meal):

- Something unique about our part of the country.
- Something unique about our town or neighborhood.
- Something weird and wonderful about our denomination and/or church.
- Something weird and annoying about our denomination and/or church.
- Something unique and quirky about our youth ministry that I love.

KURT'S RESPONSE

Wow, that may have been the shortest chapter in the history of youth ministry book chapters. I'll keep my response short as well. A few thoughts:

- Don't throw the baby out with the bathwater. Obviously, trying to be a cookie-cutter replica of another youth ministry is a bad idea, but don't let that keep you from looking at other ministries for some best practices, principles, and ideas that you can implement in your own unique, weird youth ministry.

- Insisting on being one hundred percent unique and not learning from others (I know this isn't what Marko is proposing, but could be the mindset some would have in reaction to this content) is arrogant, ineffective, inefficient, and could actually hurt your ministry much more than help it.

- Don't live in a youth ministry silo. The body of Christ and the family of churches is too vast, too rich, too deep, and too wonderful to not tap into! Don't let your insistence on "letting your freak flag fly" keep you from networking with other youth workers or convince you that one part of the body doesn't need the other. All youth ministries, and those who lead them, from mega youth ministries numbering in the thousands to small youth groups numbering in the single digits, need to protect themselves from isolation and too much independence.

The prompts Marko provided at the end of this chapter are *fantastic*, and I'd like to add a few more:

- *What church in our area is ministering to similar types of youth but doing it in a different way? What might we learn from them?*

- *What church is ministering to a totally different type of youth, and having success? What might we learn from them?*

- *What mega-youth ministry has a reputation for being generous and sharing some of their ideas and best practices? Can we contextualize these in our own unique setting?*

Part Three

OKAY, SO...

CHAPTER 9: INTENTIONALITY MODERATED WITH FAITH AND HUMILITY

Cindy was a youth pastor and a participant in one of my coaching cohorts. She was the youth pastor in what, to my experience, would be considered a small-ish church. Cindy hadn't written any books or spoken at any youth ministry events. But she'd been living out her calling, at the same church, for many years. When I got to know her, Cindy was struggling with a yet-undiagnosed muscle condition in her legs, leaving her with less and less mobility. It was a bit of a beautiful crisis for Cindy, as she needed to rethink how she lived out her calling on a day-to-day basis.

But Cindy was a paragon of *intentionality moderated by faith and humility*. She had a passionate desire to see God work in the lives of her two or three dozen teenagers. She experimented and tried new things. But she did so with an overflowing, generous heart. In fact, the youth ministry coaching cohort Cindy was in started to refer to her as the one with the "good heart."

Cindy truly had faith, in every fiber of her being, that God was working, often despite her missteps and blunders. And Cindy clearly had a heart transformed by God and filled with humility. She had no place for control and didn't take credit for success.

Cindy eventually passed away as a result of the degenerative disease that overtook her body. But I regularly think of her and her good heart. She was and is an example to me of what a great youth worker can be.

And here's the good news: Cindy wasn't an anomaly. There are thousands of Cindys out there (women and men).

What about you? What should your response be to this little book?

Should the only result be a sense of settling, embracing a "well, I guess we are fine" attitude? Should you put on a happy face, pat yourself on the back, and hop back on the hamster wheel of "the way we've always done things"?

Please, no.

Let's start with these Bible verses as a framing for our response:

> *"But forget all that—it is nothing compared to what I am going to do. For I am about to do something new. See, I have already begun! Do you not see it?"* (Isaiah 43:18-19a, NLT—it was a Bible verse long before it was a DC Talk song).

The Lord your God is with you, the Mighty Warrior who saves. He will take great delight in you; in his love he will no longer rebuke you, but will rejoice over you with singing (Zephaniah 3:17, NIV).

Yes, my soul, find rest in God; my hope comes from him (Psalm 62:5, NIV).

God will do this, for he is faithful to do what he says, and he has invited you into partnership with his Son, Jesus Christ our Lord (1 Corinthians 1:9, NLT).

A response thread weaves through all of those verses—relax your shoulders, know that God is with you, know that the "success" of your youth ministry is God's job, not yours.

What does that look like in everyday practice?

First, be intentional about a handful of things. Now, before I describe what you should be intentional about, I want to say that I was nervous about using that word here. As soon as some youth workers see the word *intentional*, they start to gird up for another round of pushing, running fast, and trying really hard. This approach, unfortunately, puts us right back in that place of subconsciously believing that we have the power to transform teenage lives.

The word *intentional* simply refers to things done with intention, or on purpose. There's nothing in there about trying really hard. Intentionally taking a nap is hardly a behavior wrought with effort.
Instead, stop.

Be intentional about keeping your focus on Jesus.

Be intentional about noticing the glass-half-full stuff Jesus is doing in the lives of teenagers.

Be intentional about celebrating what God has done, not what you haven't done.

Be intentional about people, including teenagers.

Be intentional about listening and discernment.

And be intentional about the ways your ministry can be more intentional.

Let's be clear: Intentionality is a choice. And it's a choice that often doesn't come naturally to us, particularly in the always-more-to-be-done world of youth ministry.

Once you've slowed down enough to choose intentionality, think about how you can flesh it out with giant doses of faith and humility.

When I look back on my youth ministry efforts over three decades, I can easily see that my most faithless moments were those where I was pushing the hardest for the outcomes I thought I could control.

Some time ago I was sitting, with a handful of youth workers from one of my Youth Ministry Coaching Program cohorts, in the living room of Dr. Robert Epstein (author of the radical book *Teen 2.0*—a book that has stuff in it that I profoundly resonate with, and other stuff that I really chafe at or disagree with). We were talking about the cultural construct of our current expression of adolescence in the States, and how it's often damaging to teenagers. Knowing that he had two sons from his first marriage who were twenty-seven and twenty-nine years old, and that he had a second set of children from his second marriage who ranged from five to twelve years old, I asked him how he had changed his approach to parenting. He casually dropped a bomb that has reordered my parenting and my approach to youth ministry.

He said something like, "I've moved from parenting by control to parenting by facilitation, where facilitation means identifying and nurturing competencies."

Whoa. Stop and think about that one for a moment.

So many of my efforts at youth ministry have been, if I'm really honest, about attempting to control teenagers. That sounds harsh, and I'm sure I would have put it in more Christian terms. I was structuring a clear pathway of discipleship. Or I was making sure teenagers had a firm grasp of important doctrine. Or I was making sure my volunteer team clearly understood my expectations.

Where was faith in all that? Where were my dependence on God and my belief that God was the one doing the transformation work in the lives of teenagers?

A youth ministry anchored in faith is openhanded. It's not riddled with judgment ("I'm not open to input because I don't need it") or cynicism ("Who needs hope when you have the right program?") or fear ("What will happen to me if I don't succeed?").

A youth ministry anchored in faith believes that God is at work.

And then there's that little gnat of humility. We sure have enough arrogance in the world of youth ministry. And before you quickly let yourself off the hook by claiming, "But I'm a nobody in the world of youth ministry," take stock of how you respond to successes and failures.

If you think successes and failures are mostly about you, then you've got some growth opportunities.

I'm preaching to myself here. I led countless small groups where I thought it was my brilliance that brought about a fantastic spiritual conversation, or where I thought I blew it because nothing happened beyond farts and giggles. I planned hundreds of events and mission trips and camps and retreats where my primary takeaway was either "I made that great thing happen" or "I stunk up that one."

Humility is like faith in this way: I can't make myself have it. Sure, I can desire it. And I can make conscious choices to point me in the right direction. But ultimately, humility (like faith) is something only God can birth in me.

In a somewhat strange, double-dipping way, I only become more humble when I have the humility to ask God to make me more humble.

But don't wrap up this book thinking your to-do list now includes, in addition to all the other overwhelming stuff on it, three more items (intentionality, faith, humility). I don't want to heap stuff on you! I want to encourage you and allow you to rest. My hope is that you'll experience the freedom of your calling, rather than the stress of expectations. My prayer is that you'll say to yourself, "Yup, I can do this another day, because this is God's deal, not mine."

And that's just it: There are so many faithful, humble youth workers out there. Maybe you're one of them. There's so much wonderful and beautiful and Jesus-y stuff taking place in and through youth workers like you. And the water in that *more than* half-full glass? It's the Living Water—and drinking it, you will never thirst again.

KURT'S RESPONSE

I have to admit, I love the word intentional. And I especially love the way Marko describes it as simply doing things on purpose. You might even think of it as—wait for it—being purpose-driven. (Sorry, I couldn't resist and I know that little joke will drive him crazy!)

Because Marko is the wise, guru-like sage full of spiritual depth and wisdom who smokes cigars and travels the world hanging out with youth workers, he gets to be the one who reminds you of all the fantastically powerful and very valid places we need to be intentional. I don't disagree with any of the items on his list.

And because I'm the highly pragmatic, overly enthusiastic achiever (if you are into the Enneagram, I'm a tie between a 7 and a 3; if you are into StrengthsFinder, my top five strengths are strategic, maximizer, positivity, futuristic, and ideation) who finds himself grinding it out in the local church day after day (and being somewhat resentful of Marko's life), I get to be the one to remind you of a few other things you would be wise to be intentional about. Stuff that may not matter to you, but probably matters to the church you serve. (Pro tip: you serve your church, it doesn't serve you.)

Be intentional about paying attention to what your church deems important in youth ministry. Hitting the mark in those areas frees you up to do a bunch of other stuff you may deem more important.

Be intentional about students' safety. Their physical and emotional safety must be your highest concern.

Be intentional about an overall ministry philosophy and strategy. Your strategy doesn't need to fill a three-ring binder, but it should at least fill a 3x5 index card. I've learned over the years that almost nothing awesome and amazing happens completely by accident. Part of the process of your youth ministry becoming what you hope (and what God wants) it to become is doing the hard work of strategizing, planning, and preparing.

Be intentional about appearances and perception. Galatians 1:10 (see megachurch "attractional" youth pastors can use the Bible!) reminds us of the danger of being more concerned with people-pleasing than God-pleasing, but don't use it as an excuse to be unconcerned with how you are perceived as a leader, a pastor, and a shepherd of teenagers. If you find yourself constantly defending your lifestyle, appearance, ministry climate, leadership decisions, etc., you have two appropriate choices: take heart and adjust where you feel nudged by the Holy Spirit, or find another church in which to minister that is more likely to embrace your approach to life and ministry.

In closing, I'm sad I didn't find an opportunity to climb up on my "attractional vs. missional" soapbox (hint: they go hand-in-hand and are both necessary for healthy youth ministry). Maybe I'll write a book about it and ask Marko to add the commentary!

APPENDIX

A HOMEWORK ASSIGNMENT

Skim back through the six values that great youth ministries embrace. Here: I'll make it easy for you and list them here, along with their one-sentence summaries:

THE LONG VIEW

The humble youth worker knows and lives a ministry approach that actively practices faith in God to transform lives, knowing we are powerless to change hearts.

THE POWER OF SMALL

Since small churches often don't have the resources to develop impressive programs fueled by amazing technology, they are often forced to "settle" for the core of what really works in youth ministry: a caring Jesus-following adult engaging a small group of teenagers.

THE ROLE OF THE HOLY SPIRIT

Great youth ministries are more responsive than proactive, more about discernment than planning, all with a keen ear to the unique guidance of the Holy Spirit.

INTEGRATION OVER ISOLATION

We'll see long-term faith more often when we work to decrease the constant ghettoization of teenagers and help them find meaningful belonging in the life of the church.

EMBRACING THE ROLE OF PARENTS

Great youth ministries are passionate about helping parents—the key influence on teenage faith—succeed in their God-given roles.

CONTEXTUALIZATION

In an age of splintered youth culture, great youth ministries have discerned an approach to ministry that is wonderfully unique to their context.

I'd like to suggest that you personalize this page and write some notes on it. First, identify one of the six values that you and your youth ministry are already doing pretty well. Sure, there's likely room for improvement on that value, but a little pat on the back for one of them would be good right now.

Then, identify one or two of the six that you'd like to address with strategy and action in your ministry, because you can clearly see how moving the needle on those one or two values will make a big difference in the vibrancy and impact of your ministry. Come up with a few action steps for each of those (or, ideally, gather a small group of your leaders and do this work together).